D0291008

NSW

Love's Compass

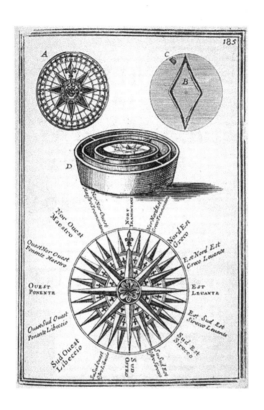

Poems by Cheryl A. Rice

Kung Fu Treachery Press

Rancho Cucamonga, CA

Copyright © Cheryl A. Rice, 2019

First Edition1 3 5 7 9 10 8 6 4 2

ISBN: 978-1-950380-76-3

LCCN: 2019955198

Design, edits and layout: John T. Keehan, Jr.

Cover image: Cheryl A. Rice

Author photo: Dayl Wise

All rights reserved. No part of this publication may be reproduced or transmitted in any form or by any means, electronic or mechanical, including photocopying, recording or by info retrieval system, without prior written permission from the author.

Acknowledgments:

"Breasts"- *Calling All Poets* 20th Anniversary Anthology

"From The Ashes"- *Egypt,* 2001: Flying Monkey Press

"Love's Compass"- *Coast to Coast,* 2011: Flying Monkey Press

"Making Love"- *Chronogram*

"Napoleon's Kiss"- *Poetalk*

"Romeo in July"- *Hobo Camp Review*

"We Have All Been There"- *Chronogram*

"You Could See"- *Home Planet News*

"You Let Me"- *Coast to Coast,* 2011: Flying Monkey Press

TABLE OF CONTENTS

From The Ashes / 1

Anticipating Stars / 2

Burning / 4

Romeo In July / 5

Landscape / 7

Making Love / 8

Drowning / 9

Morning Has A Life Of Its Own / 11

We Have All Been There / 13

You Let Me / 16

Napoleon's Kiss / 18

Finding Orion / 20

Love's Compass / 22

Fred Allen Died On St. Patrick's Night / 25

You Could See / 27

Tongue / 28

LM / 30

Graduation / 32

Joy Ride / 36

War Bonnet / 39

Her Husband's Funeral / 41

Paris Again / 43

Ellie / 45

A Shoe Drops / 46

Breasts / 38

Miata / 50

Ponies / 52

Smoker / 54

Soy Milk / 56

Bones In The Museum / 58

Mall / 60

My Vietnam / 65

-for Michael-

From The Ashes

Beetles mate and lay eggs under the charred bark... -NPR Radio

The radio says beetles thrive in fire's aftermath,
seek out charred remains of flora
in which to begin the next generation,
cuddle under smudgy beds of brittle bark.

I feel the same each time I crawl
from the wreck of another romance,
recall the sparks, branches crashing after fire
retires back to the sky.

The sun is too much in the morning,
too much trouble to follow another bug,
shell buff and gleaming.
Yet here I am again, six feet on the ground,
dragging this exoskeletal trunk
in search of creature comfort.

I find you, fellow crawler,
brilliant black wings sagging,
Phoenix of beetles rising from the ashes.
I find the will, look for a choice log
fresh with the scent of recent burn.

We will make a fire there,
drive out damp blessing of rain,
for thunder is where life begins.

Anticipating Stars

Five-point spice the star
of all this tofu,
my luck begins on
a small, windblown bridge,
ghost of wood, bones of steel,
striking parks in the creek,
Yankees in the Bronx
losing again without us,
victory dripping thru mitts.

Like you, water, dusty sun
allow curacao in our
refreshments their melancholy
after-effects, bean sprout bite,
enough chlorophyll to
trample ennui in its
arrogant Euro clogs.

We wind thru the water,
old mule trails.
Your words point my eyes
into every sharp curve.
Like the back of your hand,
you still recall a hike up
another path, picnics past,
babies sprouting common as bean pods
in the snow of your heart.

The sun, a star, too, shaves a hole
in the overcast at last,
sparks on water leap basketball heights,
the moon my tool, a swim in the middle
for the hell of it, to feel mud
on my bruised soles, rocks beneath.

Back down, dull eyes to sky,
fat lily, white star of folding, I wallow.
You take the shore, distant token.
I spin in this green soup arcade.
Take my keys! My mortgage!
I will wash in these woods,
fade into this red shore.
Take my car, please!

Cold and delighted, your ember arms
solid in my days of snaky quarters,
lavender rinse, you are real,
good, your touch a magical crack
that makes stars flicker and blush,
Your kiss in the black myrrh of these woods
an ivy to stay for, train to my limbs,
vapid frame, recall on other planets,
other dips in the down.

Burning

All who pass thru the portals
of your chamber of love
leave seared signatures,
endless burning for the rest
of your natural life.
Some are trick candles,
that can't be extinguished
with a blow or wet fingers,
others like flickering votives,
dim bulbs safe for Christmas displays,
but some few glow like fantastic fireworks,
sulfurous yellow heaps
smoldering, terminal ash.

These last are the ones that mark you,
that begin with such flash,
deafen with promise of loyalty, happily forever.
Sparks trail after kisses
of considerable skill,
intricate future plans illuminate
nights between constellations.
Too hot, too quick to last,
flesh melts at these temperatures.
Bodies cool. Spent sticks, tissues
drift away, pushed into corners
by a breeze that returns when the blast subsides.

The body is marked then in the only way
forever is possible.

Romeo in July

It's hard to be Romeo after a day in the shop,
smelling of tires, black polyester work shirts, exhaust,
hard to keep awake in the trailer's dim lamplight.
Martha Stewart in reruns
declares her pumpkin spoonbread good
in her helpful, lackluster tones.
It's challenging, Manny, Moe, and Jack aside,
to work up a spark, but you did,
our long times apart a gasoline,
igniting our few short hours together, alone.

It's no picnic either to be Juliet without poison,
long drives after cubical captivity,
Great Gildersleeve riding shotgun,
Jack Benny soothing poor, frightened Carmichael
back in the rumble seat;
Juliet without a nurse either
to run interference while I
slip into something easier
to take off later,
Juliet who has learned by now
to distinguish the Barrymores
from the understudies.

We are Juliet of the Ample Belly,
Romeo of the Hand-Rolled Smokes.
Thruway our balcony, our masquerade ball consists
of a video, chicken fingers, microwave popcorn.
The perfume of our wobbly romance is
the aroma of discount sandalwood
burning in a dollar store candle.
Wooden fish dangle from curtain rods,
your blue eyes hover in the bedroom's ocean,
rimmed with sleep, slip to the edge of our cotton stage,
no encores for this performance,
the merciful knife of night
ending our drawn out scene.

Landscape

I run my fingers down the curve of his back.
His Twins burst into squawls every few minutes
while Japanese demons tumble across the hot TV screen.
Here, snow is a given.

I travel his body every chance I get.
On this visit, I make a point to
memorize the paths of his belly,
three-day promontory of beard,
stormy grey locks that sing as he shovels.

Every few weeks we reach out our hands
and pull out the lungs of the dark,
after the Twins have fallen asleep,
before the glow of nightly calls has faded.

The snow, like our love, is steady,
scattered, drifts into piles,
uncovers bare spots,
both chills in despair, blankets in comfort.

The sun surrenders up its own good face across our land
when we least expect the light.

Making Love

As if love was a thing that could be created,
constructed of cookies or pipe cleaners,
or earned like a Blue Stamp premium.

As if when we kiss, my heart
slips out on the sly from
between my lips, thru yours,
to take a deep bite
of your extensions.

We did not create this love.
We found it, looking at the same window,
me looking out, you looking over
at land that's always been.

Our time to travel this is now,
to enjoy our common path,
not the view, dread the sunset,
the first star's debut.

Drowning

Drowning, each word over the phone
a wave licking my dry shore.
I resist, reluctant to be
consumed by his wet voice.

Between calls, I make appointments,
prepare elaborate meals,
close the shade over the kitchen sink
that he raises at every visit
to gauge the weather by the
simple appearance or disappearance
of the Catskills nearby.

As I finish the dishes, hands gloved in suds,
I remember a motel, the tongues
he spoke in stilted ecstasy, my mouth
at the source of so much life,
effort to dream ourselves into
twenty-four more hours.

Circling the lipstick bathtub,
weak-hearted anemones
nod with steam late in the night.
I try to be present fully,
taste the hereafter in his breast,
let his workday stubble grind off winding miles.

I left my arms open, hair uncombed
to search in the dark for its summer wave,
the door ajar for someone's expected escape.

His light bones bear me up over these hills,
sentimental, how high the moon, Les Paul?
Break me on the mountain's peak
and I will grow again, whole,
ear, nose, tail rising.
Time is as unkind as the tides,
sands surrounding an island of days,
slow Zen fizz to the next step of love.

Morning Has A Life Of Its Own

You linger at a shop
for a smoke and a look at
the print on display,
a Twenties couple waltzing
on a rainy beach, their
respective servants sheltering each step
with his and hers umbrellas,
discreetly oblivious to romance in motion.

We dodge raindrops like bullets
in my usual Albany weather,
the Capitol's rain gods happy
to bless me with their wet bounty.
You, more real than any Grimm prince,
wear the tie that is my gift,
fine worm floss I chose for
its watery weave, and the
excellent pond it provides
for your old gold tie tack,
fish out of fin no more.

You and I don't curse the rain, or fear it.
We prefer the patter of its stories
on a roof, above our lingering heads,
but night goes fast, morning
has a life of its own.

We flow with a kind
of concentrated love.
Your mouth slips too quick to my heart.
Fingers dapple the seconds onto my back
until we have worked the daylight
up behind the blinds.

You dance your best in the
foot charts I arrange, rearrange,
to irregular rhythms of my blood's river.
Rain for us is an art, like love.
The weight of days passed alone
lightens in your salty aspects,
blue calm, saturated shore.

We Have All Been There

-for Lisa Nowak

We have all been there—
festering anxiety, sudden split,
the 'let's be friends' routine,
training together for the spring regatta
because it's already paid for.

We've all made the horrid discovery,
emails, someone else's lipstick
on a beer can, moon boots not your size
drying in the garage.

We've all been on that frantic journey,
diapered in body or spirit because
you're saving the shit for the one who deserves it,
not the Quickie Mart cashier, toll taker,
or your kids, the poor bastards,
you'll spend more time with them
after all this is settled,

and certainly not your loving,
Earthbound spouse.
You loved him once, but there's no common ground now.
You can't share anything about
the clarity of the Milky Way when you're
RIGHT THERE. You can't explain it.

There's no going back.

We've all had our showdowns,
empowered by false nose, fright wig or
greasepaint moustache.
We've all needed just to talk,
to explain how he or she is the world to you,
flawed and fragmented as it is,
how angry you are at the way
it all turned out, your mixed-up plans,
how Texas will feel for the rest
of your life, how Earth
won't be big enough again
for the three of you.

We have all arrived here on the worst possible roads,
behaved worse than even our biggest fans would ever believe.
We leave judgment to the tabloids,
who never get the story straight.
They never write about his promises
in deep, weightless night,
three years of hiding from the stars,
letting yourself in the back door,
fresh scent of his cotton sheets.

No, the so-called reporters only talk about
the isolated meltdown, steel mallet,
National Geographics tied with kitchen twine,

half a tuna sandwich wrapped in plastic,
teeth bare to pepper spray and all threats.

Nobody cares about the end of the story,
the stunted career, quiet divorce.
The moon is the only constant,
unphased, sticking to schedule.
We have all been there, and
they don't call lovers 'lunatics'
for nothing.

You Let Me

You let me go, back then,
but today you wrap me in your
trench coat love,
big as I remember,
grey in my heart mirrored
in your beard of many colors.

Grounded in sugared caffeine now,
making love would be easy.
All the corners in this town
I looked for your ghost on,
those backward glances I longed to tame,
that sit with us now, content,
as I let my tea steep
black as our love,
and your club soda,
bubble by bubble, buys us time.

I carried your memory,
lucky penny in my shoe,
to lift me over the patches,
finally, to belated electronic thanks.
Did you ever think you'd see us again?
It's good to have one love to come back to
in this life of packing boxes, immovable dressers,
return addresses never returning.

It is good to have an old love to come home to,
fingertip stories and an understanding kiss.
That penny rings under my foot,
elevated savior,
pure secret holder of hands.

Napoleon's Kiss

You wait in the wings
as I make my entrance,
remove my black wool with a flourish.
You know, sooner or later,
I will come to you.
Head sparsely flocked,
chin precisely trimmed,
you are entirely the same.
Black is as black does,
decipherable shadow of indecision.

You try to surround me like
a lamb of little consequence gone astray.
I sit. You sit. I walk,
you limp beside me,
wounded, overripe pup.
We perch on separate couches,
peck at the same shrimp platter.
You are at my heel in every room,
as I glad hand the holidays
one palm at a time.
Even out of my sight,
I feel your breath in my periphery.
You arms paw clumsily,
and at last, on the stairs,
you snag for a moment the bit of me
that's ashamed to be pleased.

I regret your kiss, desired
from the moment I arrived,
the moment we met, and even now,
see no future in it, only
the bitter tongue that speaks
its own warped truths.
I loved you, you insist,
your hand tugging mine for emphasis.
You did, in the only way you know.

I remind you about the one you chose.
You stumble, sigh, tired of your story, too.
I rewrap, adjust the faux mink caressing my neck
before I return to the deep, narcotic night,
Orion and his bum heal laughing, limping.

Finding Orion

I can slay any beast on earth!
he boasts to Artemis, who
often joins him in the hunt,
prowls the forest by moonlight or torches,
plays by his simple rules.

Barefoot but for a hero's sandals,
Mother Earth tires of his rough shenanigans,
sends the only creature to challenge him
that he's long dismissed.

The scorpion's vintage elixir
bursts quickly thru his veins.
His distracted heel swells after just one strike,
straps of his sandals split.

He waits now for boots to be reinvented,
clings to his solid brass club,
paperweight in the book of night.

Orion's belt of three bright queens
points towards speckled Sirius,
radio dog start, unbreakable weapon at hand.
He lords it over the other stars,
still the Mighty Hunter,
his game gone South.

Train your eyes southwest to find him,
or northwest, if you're south,
or merely west if you're at the Equator,
for he is a giant.
It's easiest though to find Orion at dawn,
or in the evening. Like all men,
he is full of contradictions.

Love's Compass

I let him find me first,
afraid he's changed, that I
won't recognize him,
I stare at the TV above the coffee counter, wait.
He touches my shoulder.
I know him right away, his touch,
neatly buttoned shirt pressed
briefly against me, groomed details
befitting a man in public service.

After we sit, receive our coffee,
I let him go on about the economy,
recent elections, politics his thing.
I soak up his familiar face,
clipped beard, unwavering eyes,
as his big hand chops the air
between us for emphasis,
then reaches for mine,
stops short at my fingertips.

Fried eggs before us, bacon for garnish,
whole wheat toast a nod to middle age,
bowl of creamers on the table
deep enough to sink the Titanic.
Some music wanders in the background,
but it isn't our song.

It's never our song.

The where or when of us in ancient history,
distant as the day we met.
I sprouted legs, and crawled onto your shore.
This breakfast is merely a wake,
two old friends celebrating invisible beauty,
intangible times.

He is transplanted to a land of
orange groves, jumping skulls.
I am tethered to this valley of shallow, green graves.
The man I live with keeps one eye on the bedpost,
is deeply handsome, delicious from stem to core.

But I am in love with this moment here, too,
with breakfast, the past,
a pure passion I have never satisfied,
yet have outgrown.

When we part, again,
we hug long and deep,
exchange outlaw kisses.
I understand now how all things imagined obstacles
can be navigated with love's compass.
New territory would now be part of the journey,
not a reason to avoid the exploration.

The woman I am today
waits until she's in the car,
windows rolled up, AC on high,
before she cries, feeling nothing
but precisely kicked in the gut,
pancakes no cushion to the blow.
For years I wondered why Rick let Ilsa go,
why Streisand and Redford
couldn't make it work.
The rich, the ill-advised might keep reaching,
spend a lifetime grabbing at gold rings,
carousal turning despite our best intentions.

I have a man at home who's
been to weddings, funerals with me.
Firings and late bills fill the cracks between us,
and if not till death, we'll get close enough.
Without worry or fear, he is the home
I was meant to be in,
the touch that landed me
in the best of all possible adventures.

Fred Allen Died on St. Patrick's Night

Fred Allen died on St. Patrick's night, 1956, not,
as legend has it, walking his dog, but taking his
customary stroll around Manhattan.
He'd been in failing health for some time,
and the next night, "What's My Line," the
TV show he'd been a panelist on for the two
years before, carried on, as per the wishes
of his wife, Portland.

Today I'd be hard-pressed to find
someone my age who knows who Fred Allen was,
where Allen's Alley might have been found
on the radio dial, not people my age.
His books were best sellers, but his best known
pen pal, Groucho Marx, is the one remembered,
and even he is fading into just a rubber nose and
glasses, gag gift made in China, these days
missing the moustache and cigar.

The only scrap of immortality that remains
of Fred Allen's lengthy career, beginning in
vaudeville, through radio, TV, a movie or two,
and some very funny books, is a chicken.
One of the Alley's residents was a blowhard
senator from somewhere south of the Mason-
Dixon, Senator Claghorn by name. He was
loud and phony and full of flowery phrases,
the kind you'd expect from a politician.

I say there- I say, boy! You know the
phrase, because Warner Brothers
stole it, along with the persona, for their
Foghorn Leghorn, a tribute to Allen,
before the days of lawyers and nitpicking,
when tributes were possible.

Everyone remembers the chicken,
but not the ham who outlived vaudeville,
grew too sick to stroll the Alley,
who died on a walk around the block
St. Patrick's night,
long after the parade had passed by, and
long before it was thought necessary to
dye the beer and bagels green.

I mention Fred Allen because even he,
with millions of fans across the country,
around the English-speaking world, could
not out-distance our old friend Death, even
at a brisk pace down West 57th.

Although we'd like some to stay forever,
it is reassuring to remember that eventually
all will go the same way, whether on a
stroll, sleeping peacefully or even
choking on a chicken bone. We have
that to hold onto. There's light
at the end of this alley, too.

You Could See

for Donald Lev

As he leaned into the Blade of Time,
you could see how he whittled himself down
to bone & word, how his poems became
ninja stars, tender, perfect points.

You could see year after year,
as clothes slid from his body, his belt
tighten, loose ends dangling like sash of
a Zen master's robes, how his two legs became
three, the newest of hobbled wood.

You could see brain and body parting ways,
reluctant divorce, but still the Blade, burnished
words shining in our ears. We had no right to
beg for more.

Tsunami of poems trickled to a
thin stream of blood, our hands left full of
evaporated skin, the Brooklyn Dodgers, a tulip,
a full cup to toast the man who beat back the Blade.

Tongue

During my latest round of March madness,
annual time when my life force tries its damndest
to leave my body behind, my tongue has decided
to get into the act, lifting from my mouth
like a piece of cold corned beef,
fissures down the center that may or may not be
the beginnings of some grander scheme of obsolescence.
A vague soreness on its ragged Apollo surface
matches that of my mouth's roof,
smooth where there should be texture,
rough where there now is molten flesh.

A night's sleep leaves it desiccated,
temporarily revived by a cup of tea, a vegetable smoothie,
as has become my morning eye opener,
my eyes on the horizon now
for Eostre the moonlit hare's slow leap
to correct our circumstances,
bring resurrection back to my forsythias,
dormant under rocky pads of snow.

I am trying yoga this year, steam, and poetry,
a kind of prayer, to bring myself back into the fold,
tongue, fingers, follicles intact,
to meet the green season with some degree of dignity,
half a lung, half a lung,
not yet ready to honor the ancestors
with my presence.

LM

I wake my mother from her afternoon nap
to ask for a dime.
Groggy, she digs it out of her purse,
and I tape it to a postpaid card.
Soon, the model arrives, Lunar Module that
had landed a few weeks before on the moon,
five inches high when completed.
I am not a model builder, or even an aspiring astronaut.
Women since Amelia Earhart can barely hope to fly,
much less leave the atmosphere, weightless,
dependent on tanks for air,
tubes for dinner.

That first walk is
broadcast late at night.
Despite the history, my parents
don't let us stay up to watch.
It's summer, no excuse like
getting up for school applies.
I am seven, my sister five and a half,
my brother just turned three.
Later, he becomes the stargazer in the family,
rootless, following the sun,
Hollywood Boulevard his landing strip.

Maybe the memory of that first Apollo
is still too vivid for them,
three astronauts lost to oxygen's raging flames.
Tragedy's a constant in the '60s,
a given on the Nightly News.
I remember David Brinkley's report in front of
the charred remains of that first mission.

After my model arrives, a new book a month comes,
once-a-month science in slender soft covers
that fit in the same slipcovered case.
I never finish the model,
skim the books without much interest.
I missed the fine print on that postcard,
thought a single dime would open up
the universe to me, postpaid.
I thought for a moment that
I too could fly, wings spread
wide over the Everglades,
uterus forgiven.

Graduation

Note the high-tension lines above our heads,
the empty stalls over my shoulder.
This is where I grew,
last gasp of rural Long Island,
street unpaved just twenty years before,
barns and corrals filled with
amateur horses, a few pretenders
back and forth to Belmont,
but overall pleasure seekers
rambling down the wide off-street paths.
Our house beside a large corral
filled with a revolving herd
of boarders, nibbling bits of green
that crept over from our unkempt yard
into the dust of their domain.

In the picture, it's June.
I know this because I am wearing
my graduation dress, Chinese style
in a glossy blue-grey fabric
that catches the late day light,
accents my curves, and the
gold piping at my throat.

My grandmother's with me,
hair done for the occasion
in the bouffant she'd be buried in
seven years later.

I am thrilled to be finished,
sorry to leave all the friends
I think I'll keep forever,
oblivious to the diaspora of college,
marriage, life. Grandma,
whom we called Grandma Mi,
looks on with pride,
first grandchild to complete high school,
headed to college, but still,
I lack her skill with
pans and platters, can barely
make oatmeal, let alone
the fabulous roasts and fancies
she offers up, Grossingers
her culinary educator.

I see now a frailty in her complexion,
diabetic glow that would wear her down
completely so soon after,
the bullish body that served as her best tool
coming slowly apart, hands that once gripped
whisk and knife beginning their swift descent to stillness.
I see now the mortality I didn't think possible.

There is a car behind us, not mine,
and inside the small house a cake,
a few relatives who will drift, too,
cousins who will also graduate,
go on to colleges across the country,
accidental veins connecting us drawn thin,
breaking as prejudices, inborn inclinations take hold.

I leap off to college, and my life does change,
despite my father's well-intended warning
about how it's a *man's world,*
and part of it is, but not the
part I was interested in.
Those men of power without soul,
money without the notion to do interesting things,
those men I avoid.
I learn to cook, could already sew,
find my driving mojo later.
I fill my own barns with
stallions of my choosing,
reassign stalls as needed.
High tension is a way of life,
but not in the way I was raised to believe.

Grandma Mi, short for a long European name
that maybe my parents feared
too much for our small tongues to bear,
struck out on her own early on, too,
armed with just a spoon, her strong body,
and a weakness for bakers and some sort of punishing god.

She covered her head on those rare occasions
she attended church with us,
easy-going Lutheran affair that cared not
about transgressions or lace, left you to confess
your own true sins in private.

I leave my head bare, even
when protection would be more prudent.
I leave my head bare, my
strong hands exposed to all the elements
this world has to throw at me.

Joy Ride

Through the magical internet,
I see the temperature in Atlanta is 45 degrees,
raining, comfortable for a recount.
Here in upstate New York,
starless sky above, we brace for
winter's first real snow.
The supermarket's out of toilet paper,
bottled water, Pop Tarts,
but I've planned ahead.
I quit Pop Tarts years ago,
the night I left my husband in broad daylight,
no trail of crumbs, no way to find me.

I know how you voted, my Jersey girl,
marooned in the South for love
of the only man I've met who
might deserve your devotion.
The weather is warmer than here, brutal,
some might call it, but despite my father's
never-ending jokes,
the snow upstate always melts.
We have our seasons of sauna,
when my Beloved and I lap up
precious drops of mechanical coolness
here in the cottage we call home.

You know who I voted for, too.
I am without regret, comfortable
in this illusive cocoon,
thugs in Albany still saying
everything I want to hear,
taxes not much for my little house,
my needs so few beyond some select books,
one good computer, and
a car that starts up every morning.

For our 50th birthdays, we compromised,
meeting in D.C. for a long weekend
of sight-seeing, fine dining,
touring the national treasures
in December's bitter wind.
In the open-air top of a double-decker,
we spun around the city, our bare heads
snapping and shivering as we
passed all the landmarks we'd
not find time to visit.

At the Lincoln Memorial,
I glanced at the statue,
but took more encouragement
from the faces of those who'd come
to pay their respects to Abraham.
They glowed with an awe I was
unaccustomed to, a reverence.

They came from everywhere,
each adding their dialect
to the melting pot voices
rolling around that hall,
spilling into the long pond
still deep with Martin's elegant oration.

I am afraid to return to the Capitol these days,
 afraid I will get myself arrested or worse,
pass blithely by the house of our leader
without remark.
I am afraid for our golden years
spent not in meadows of loosestrife,
sunsets falling behind the Gunks,
enough Technicolor for everyone's dreams,

but in the streets, crocheting crazy hats
meant to taunt the powers that be,
remind them of the power of pussies
unbound by tiny hands and tiny minds.
I like to think I'm ready to die by now after all,
for this, for another turn of evolution's wheel,
but I like my ibuprofen a little too much.
I like that the furnace kicks on at my bidding,
can't imagine what one more poem might accomplish,
but I keep writing, in times of war or peace.
Will I have the marbles left to memorize my work if
the New Nazis come for my papers?
If I do, all the better, for going down that slippery slope
will be all the more joyful with my wits,
my words about me.

War Bonnet

In a dim, distant wing of the Royal Ontario Museum,
Sitting Bull's war bonnet rests beside his deer skin shirt,
poster-sized photo of him overlooking all.
Nothing to see here, I snarl to invisible throngs.
'Just the remains of another dirty Indian,' the message implicit.

I know this chief well, at least by sight.
His portrait hung in our living room when I was growing up.
My father clipped his image from the Sunday paper,
glued it to a wooden board he'd hammered and stained
to resemble a Western artifact.

There is more to the story than fits on an index card.
This chief surrendered these treasures willingly for sanctuary,
his own and a small band of loyal followers.
They lived in wild Manitoba four restless years,
rent paid with precious eagle feathers,
each earned with honor, sacrificed for safety.

The bonnet's at ease now, golden feathers that
once stood straight like rays of sun now
limp with age despite the Great Chief's spirit,
confirmed by descendants, in these common molecules.

I can't say whether that family plaque
survived my parents' exodus to Florida.
My father's as old now as the chief was in our portrait.
His childhood lunch box, Hopalong Cassidy, was left behind,
full of nails and rust, in his own father's basement.

My father's teeth, worn smooth as a dolphin's,
are useless now for mashing sinews into useable laces.
The soles of his moccasins grown slick and thin,
there is nowhere left for him to run,
his own long war almost over.

Her Husband's Funeral

It's become routine now.
The open hole in the earth doesn't frighten me
nearly as much as an empty bed.
The new widow raises her arms,
wraps us in her intricate shawl
woven of fibers she picked herself.
For the moment, her grief is manageable.
We gather in near silence,
her husband's Eastern faith
so all-encompassing that
only one prayer is needed,
and she is his priest.

* * *

It is not the death of a body
that makes me doubt a universal order.
It is the sudden shift of a love from gingerbread dreams,
house plastered with wedding photos,
anniversary plans six months ahead,
to a new orbit, out of the path
I'd grown comfortable with,
old constellations seismically shattered.
We'll help this other carry her things to a new apartment,
greet her soon-to-be ex with awkward tears,
not my marriage, not my breaking.
We will follow her lead, comet already on fire.

* * *

By the time I get to the funeral,
the deceased has already been carried out.
I imagine his gentle form
wrapped in linens, unpreserved,
laid carefully in a box of plain poplar,
waiting to rejoin the earth we began in.

* * *

My heart waits breathless for my turn to be abandoned,
long past possessing fire to do the leaving, or the need.
There were times I burned house after house down,
seeking an orbit of my own, ground too sifted,
too dry to sustain my liquid being.
All worlds collide this week, past and present,
like thunder overhead as funeral prayers are finished,
as bridges are burned by a younger star
yearning for a fresh heaven.

Paris Again

When you find yourself saying, 'Oh, it's Paris again,'
you know it's time to stop, I overhear a woman say,
long past a life of movement and flight.

I have never had a great desire to see the world.
Rather, I go somewhere to see things—
a particular painting, a singer, family.

All else, the homes, the food,
even the basic features of the supposed foreigners
strike me as all too familiar,
hardly worth the effort.

My brother went to Paris once, years ago.
I never got many details.
I know he wanted to recreate the famous photo
of the couple kissing quickly, stolen on the street.
He was unsuccessful.

I can't imagine what's left for me
of Henry Miller's Paris, in any case,
dirty garrets, soft touches and bare stick flats
that filled that city between the streets and bridges
he walked so often, sometimes hard to tell from
halcyon Brooklyn streets he writes about, too.

And yet, and yet—I am supposed to want to go to the trouble.
Even so, says that woman who'd sworn it off,
there's no place like it in the world.
Paris returns again, myth and martyr,

and I wonder if I too am really done with my travels.

Ellie

I am fifty-five and a half, you less than one.
I urge you on, my ambassador to the future.
You'll see things, for better or worse,
I can't imagine, as I saw

Cuban missiles hover at Florida's shores,
the Mets win two world series after a rocky birth,
three assassinations that poisoned
the candied waters of peaceniks,
threw us into disco melodramas,
the World Trade Center built, demolished, canonized.

All this my family before me could not have imagined,
as their ancients could never have imagined Hitler,
as we could never have imagined his return.
I encourage you to hold hands with
your next-door love, feed the dog, make sure
the birds have water, breathe in the direction
of sky, of tomorrow, where the winds
must take us all.

A Shoe Drops

We watched "The Last Waltz" last week on Netflix
and I'd never seen it before, but I saw Rick Danko once—
in a diner in Woodstock, both gone.
This style of man is the yardstick by which
all other times in my life are measured.
Slight, pointed collars, corduroy bell bottoms,
cigarettes, the dreaded cigarettes punctuating sentences,
but everyone smoked and only
half of them are dead now.

My aunt had George Harrison's first solo effort.
I loved the cover, not glossy like the others,
George squatting in a wizard's soft hat,
surrounded by garden gnomes I didn't know yet
were not exotic, but the most domestic of
English garden creatures.
It was the time when Yoko was blamed for everything.

Old West style the fashion, sepia photos, guitars
rolling together like waves in a roaring brook, each
taking a turn, steady drumbeat ruffling the waters,
adding chew to the savory texture, and it sunk into me.
At heart, I am a flower child, though tie dye distracts
from the awkward lines of my rounded body.
I gave up guitar a long time ago, fingers too short
to make it matter, no music pouring from me.
burning to be out on display.

I woke this morning dreaming in half sleep of a
hanging lamp my parents had in the living room
two houses ago, six-sided lantern, amber panels
of plastic that light shone through.
It was hard to leave bed, let this simple object
drift back to the Rolodex at the back of my brain.
I wonder what became of it, how it would clash
with their Florida furniture, all soft
blues and beiges, seagulls and lighthouses.

Yet my brain clings to that old lamp.
I have trouble allowing the flow, time to pass with me.
Resistance? I am in the moment and
outside all at once, taking notes for future poems,
for the stories to be told after this
movie of life is over, stories to share in
the lobby after the show.

Breasts

Among the cruel jokes between us,
slipping back and forth as lovers do
between the lands of adoration and distaste,
are ones about my unused breasts.

They've spent their lives as radiant magnets
set to test young men of my early school years,
nicknames like *Twin Towers,* meant to
joke away their fascination.

Perhaps they were adored in silence, too,
stars in someone's late, afterschool
masturbation melodrama,
my real flesh safely out of reach.

They've been appetizers as well,
good for warm-up to brief encounters,
and longer interludes,
spanked and kneaded as
playmates explored their
potential, pale pots of
Silly Putty, warm globes of iridescence
at their momentary disposal.

Biological function never triggered,
we joke about dust collecting where
milk ducts are supposed to be.
We imagine sweet clouds emerging at the
slightest squeeze, dandelions caressing their young.

There is no flavor in me that would have
satisfied an infant's hunger,
no untapped craving to sustain another life.
From the time I weaned myself,
my breasts were never here to nurse the world.

I suckled myself, completing a circuit of need,
reliance, self-made woman.

Miata

Blue as the rarest moon,
his Miata dashes past the
palms, my brother at the wheel.
Top down, temperature normal
for a Florida winter eve,
what slows us down is the toll booth,
forced weaving from lane to lane like a gater
lumbering towards a litter of poodles.

It's not New York, not even Los Angeles,
my brother's most recent haunt before this.
I didn't quit LA; LA quit me, he says, half-joking.
At home I chide my Beloved for 40 in a 35,
but tonight 80 seems right.
My hair is short enough to whip a bit,
but no unmanageable tangles form.
My brother's hair, thinning for years,
hibernates beneath a ball cap.
Neither of us are fans.

The stars appear one by one in the bluing sky,
the moon offstage, waiting for her cue.
Nobody wants to end up in Florida, says my brother,
but so he has-- family, finances, similar climate.
I've been vocally opposed to the state
for years now but some nights—

the clear, soft atmosphere clinging to the gas pumps,
ground level, intact, water, water everywhere—

I can imagine a sort of life here,
tropical suburbs fenced in by disappointment,
lives rebuilt grain by grain from sands of mortality.
His new house, surrounded by ancient chain-link
my brother reinforces with salvaged wood,
may someday enjoy a mural echoing
the barrios of East LA, or is that another joke,
oceans of promise behind us, destined for only
stain and trumpet vines and sun?

Ponies

-for Donald Lev

Donald, I think you knew the ponies best
by association, like me, not directly involved
in production and distribution
of substantial portions of your
weekly paycheck to NYRA.

There is a beauty to it unlike any other sport,
athletes garbed in a rainbow of silks,
vehicles bred like college recruits
to perform just one physical task,
but to do it better than all the others.

I'm still proud to pronounce on Trivia Night:
Palomino, Chestnut, Roan.
Trigger was a Palomino,
but never saw this kind of action,
never strolled the graceful gardens of Belmont
or took the waters in Saratoga.

The OTBs have dried up,
my father's second home,
The Office, he joked on Saturday mornings,
going in on weekends to make arrangements.
I never bet, but take guesses,
scry *The Daily Racing Form* for signs,

predict the future from what's gone before,
then drop my spare change in a jar at home,
bills in an undisclosed location.

Somewhere on the outskirts of memory,
poetry is where you and I prefer to live, Donald,
where we take our chances,
better odds, bigger pay-outs.

Smoker

When the air is heavy in July,
disguising the Catskills in smoky haze,
we smell cigarettes outside the kitchen window
though my Beloved quit years ago,
clings instead to the Chinese vapors
all the kids are going for between
impossible burgers and wheat grass shakes.

If we are feeling superstitious,
or even nostalgic, we say it's Jim,
come back from the dead
to bum another cigarette,
monthly check gone to his
basement rent, ramen, and taxis.

Jim was never bold enough
to knock on the door.
He would stand at a polite distance,
smoking his last, and hope
we would spot him, waiting.

He declined to come in,
rarely accepted a ride.
My Beloved's hand-rolled darlings
were the single indulgence he allowed himself

at the end of his life, when liver, lungs,
feet had all begun to fail.
He allowed himself the soothing caress of nicotine
to help pass the last days.

When he died, a sister we'd never met
gave the newspaper Jim's high school graduation photo
to print beside his obituary.
Handsome, smiling, thick hair neatly combed,
wide plaid lapels smooth and cheerful.
Maybe it was all she had left of him,
all she could remember,
knowing as little about the reasons for his fate,
his bad decisions, as Jim had himself.

Soy Milk

A gallon of soy milk in my fridge begins the sixth of its seven
    days of wholesomeness.
Beware, my darlings. No one will hire you of any substance after
    the age of fifty,
especially with a resume full of too many degrees, too few unions.
I fell into employment as a way to support my art, never
believing art was a way to support my lavish lifestyle of food,
    shelter, gas.

The soy milk agrees, begins a riot inside the carton, protests
    a lack of flavor.
My tongue knows not the difference between almond or cow,
sweet or sour, old or young. I thought I could merely rotate from
    shop to shop
in the great mall on the hill, now empty hulk, the very essence
    of marketing
morphed into something out of sight, sighing as a mother
    whose nest lies
empty, bare but for a desperation of new carpet, historical
    posters planted hopefully by new, improved owners.

I work at the one place that would have me, freelancing a dying art.
I've seen the somebodies hired, stumble through a year or two,
move on to paler pastures after sucking this one dry. There is a
    kind

of cancer around me too, of resignation, of nostalgia, that
    seems to
freeze most in place, despite babies, deaths, deeply held
    mistakes
coming to light. It is all I can do to keep mortgage and mind
    together,

all I can do to pass the time until one or more pensions is
    in reach.
I keep my nose to the keyboard, glance out at the changing
    light,
now winter's pale haze, now summer's blue fire.
Rain spatters the car I can't afford, but do, because
I'll need it for holidays, joy rides seeking joy, commutes
    where
I pretend I'm not going to work, but some exotic adventure
where a poet is safe, where my words will sustain me.

Bones in the Museum

Among the bones, cages in cages,
though I've been among such bones before
at various museums, freak shows, corporate headquarters,
I finally feel the burnish of centuries,
my age versus theirs, no contest,
flash on a world where I would be
overwhelmed, pound for pound,
by the fleshed-out versions
of these birds, these dogs, these harmless lizards
in their prime, all about harm,
instincts undisguised by suits and ties,
three-piece camouflage accented with
coordinating pocket square.

Instead, bones browned by years of oxygen and terror,
are only remains of a planet where
humans still wait to evolve,
where dinosaurs pass with ease
through their tropical continents.
I can see why Fundamentalists are frightened,
admire the stories they make up about a vast conspiracy,
the manufacture of giant bones to be planted around Earth,
discovered, faked, scientists in cahoots,
all in order to discredit their historical fable
about the talking snake and
a lively trilogy of founders.

It's almost too much, big, brown bones
behind UV thwarting glass,
cases scattered like the bones once were,
no rhyme, no reason, as if it all just happened,
as if the Universe had a mind of its own,
and called in sick whenever it damned well
felt like it.

Mall

I. Hudson Valley Mall

Polkas dance on the radio,
Octoberfest, a new mall,
and you & I go to look
because all we do is look,
not actually manifesting
anything like a major purchase
while we are in school,
surviving on mac & cheese,
and your parents' handouts.

We take the back roads,
me being new to the valley,
you unfamiliar to the route,
uncomfortable with the easy Thruway
and saving a few pennies
for ice cream at Friendly's later.

We pace the corridors,
Kmart with its big café in back,
apple dumplings in vanilla sauce,
Friendly's walk up window on
the main walkway, and McDonald's,
Chinese restaurant down one wing,
t-shirt store, Hallmark,
Radio Shack, and CVS for
candy and condoms.

Nothing more, and nothing less
than we can buy in our own town,
college town with supermarkets
and bookstores, drugstores and
gas stations, but it is the journey,
something we can agree on,
instead of staying home
with the radio, watching one of two
stations we get over the airways
on our black & white TV,
watching blue jays eat all of the
good seed on our porch from a
Styrofoam tray because feeders
are too costly, or tumbling in
the absence of love, building up the
courage it would take to leave.

II. Walt Whitman Mall

I'd been weaned on malls as a child,
my earliest memory rushing
from shop to shop in the Whitman Mall,
waiting for gates to open,
my mother anxious to get done
whatever she needed to do in one day,
one day with the car and the money,
and all three of us kids dressed and mobile.

Later, I'd take the bus, with friends or alone,
up Deer Park Avenue, then Jericho Turnpike,
to browse the basement at McCrory's,
buy a pretzel, throw a penny into
Macy's fountain, or count the coins
below the surface, glittering in afternoon sun.

There was a shop with Foods of all Nations,
sugar-coated violets like Grandma Mi kept
in her hutch for treats, and a Spencer's
for popular t-shirts and adult toys under
black light, for our education.
I got my *Leaves of Grass* in a small bookstore
down a side wing, quiet and empty,
and brought it with me to college,
when I crossed over, and I haven't finished yet.

III. Hudson Valley Mall, Again

Years later, after I leave you,
I apply for and get a job as
Assistant Manager at the bookstore
in the still newish mall, in a new wing
with a newfangled *food court,*
and I put the decals in the windows
on the outside, which the mall had
forbidden us to do, but nobody notices,
not the rent-a-cops patrolling the halls,
the window washers at their meditative task,
no one.

I take the paperbacks out to the
compactor after their covers have been
harvested for return credit, guard
the remains so that god forbid the
homeless, the student poor might be
inclined to reach in and snatch a book
from its steel jaws, never a problem.

And I meet a new you, a decade younger,
and we stroll through the metal beams
and raw lights, construction in progress,
then shuttle between each others' stores,
twin sons of a single corporate monster,
and new-you leaps on the hood of his car
at midnight in the parking lot, yells,
I love this woman! to whoever is listening.

And then the mall goes on without me,
then without new-you, too, and we go ahead
to other malls, other parking lots,
other strolls of works in progress.

IV. Crossgates Mall

And then grad school, because where else,
and another new-you, clad in leather,
tempered tie and polyester slacks.

My first glance is new-you carving
Dracula from Styrofoam stone,
and your waiter's closet, your Corvair style,
your life a walking Nadar warning,
unsafe at any speed, classic lines,
but no hint of which way is backwards.

Another version of McBooks,
another mall to lose myself in,
cinema, pizza joint, gourmet gift shop
where I steal electric backrubs on my lunch breaks.
Move entirely of my choice,
I chase a ghost who'd slipped over the border
as I crossed, a year of musical vehicles,
my car on the street while we take yours,
or switch sides at dawn before the cops
can leave love notes, charge us for love,
directions to your
place scribbled at midnight.

After that year, after the
emerald halls of higher learning
fade, too sterile for the life
I'm supposed to lead,
I click rubber heels,
tumble south, leave all yous
to your combustible dreams,
leave all yous in your comfortable
loop of exhaust, familiar corners
that you'd never really leave.

My Vietnam

You're all still my young uncles,
full heads of dark, wild hair, blue jeans,
olive drab fatigues from the
Army-Navy store, often barefoot.
You haven't yet quit smoking,
still drink Schaefer, haven't switched to small batch brew.
You have a hot dog once in a while on the Fourth of July,
and black bean burgers are far in the future.
None of you needs suspenders or canes.
You all recall your trusty Zippos
with fondness and disgust.
You wear your scars like medals,
uncertain pride at your achievements.

There was this Vietnam when I was a kid
for as far back as I could remember,
between episodes of *The Galloping Gourmet*
sloshing around the kitchen, charming housewives
    and sponsors
(before God found him and took away booze, pork,
and other earthly delights).
No one I knew then gone away, no wounded relatives
drinking six bullets a day to forget,
no tropical curtains drawn between us.
Our history books ended at Yalta,
Roosevelt weak and ill, cloaked in black,
that good war having spread him so thin.

Frank Blair, bulldog of the morning news,
related the facts before a hand drawn map,
poster paint continents, black dots standing in
for thousands of citizens, Hanoi, Saigon, Phnom Penh.
In Country correspondents brought the jungle
into our living room, bowl cuts, grapefruit mics,
soldiers dodging cartoon foliage,
Beany and Cecil lurking in the nearby China Sea.
A scroll of the new dead ended each broadcast.

Back then, I knew nothing about how a pink cloud
can suddenly appear where a man just stood
when a landmine is tripped.
My teenage aunt embroidered peace signs
on my jeans, barely fitting by
the time they were returned.
She wore her diamond engagement ring to work,
ringing out groceries, along with her
ragged edged jeans, bare feet saved for after hours.

You're still all my young uncles, now growing old,
textbook hippies, grey ponytails thinning,
combat boots bright with forty years polish,
soft bellies bulging under tentative hearts.
You look like the rest of us,
ophthalmologists, professors, bartenders.
You're postal workers, grandfathers,
brains wise to ticker tape festivals, confetti camouflage,
feeling your way through this gentle apocalypse,
the lie of good wars making good neighbors.

You look like my friend Dan, three-headed poet.
You look like Dayl, who gathers the living dead
into portable volumes, handy primers
for those of us only familiar with one green man,
Gumby, green as a rice paddy, of clay like
the clay that clung to combat boots,
clay like the feet of soldiers themselves,
welcomed home at last to this burning mic.

Cheryl A. Rice's poems have appeared in magazines and journals around the world. Chapbooks include *Until the Words Came* (2019: Post Traumatic Press), coauthored with Guy Reed, *Moses Parts the Tulips* (2013: APD Press), and *Lost and Found* (2019: Flying Monkey Press). She is founder/host of the now defunct "Sylvia Plath Bake-Off." Her blog is at: http://flyingmonkeyprods.blogspot.com/. Rice lives in New York's Hudson Valley.

BLACK DRAGON POETRY SOCIETY

CERTIFIED AND APPROVED

CPSIA information can be obtained
at www.ICGtesting.com
Printed in the USA
LVHW041607230220
647572LV00002B/134

9 781950 380763